Beans:

All About Them

Beans:
All About Them

by

Alvin and Virginia Silverstein

illustrated by Shirley Chan

Prentice-Hall, Inc. Englewood Cliffs, N.J.

Printed in the United States of America J

Prentice-Hall International, Inc., London
Prentice-Hall of Australia, Pty. Ltd., North Sydney
Prentice-Hall of Canada, Ltd., Toronto
Prentice-Hall of India, Private, Ltd., New Delhi
Prentice-Hall of Japan, Inc., Tokyo

Library of Congress Cataloging in Publication Data

Silverstein, Alvin.
    Beans.

    SUMMARY: Discusses beans in legend and history, how
to grow them, and their future use as a low-cost protein
supplement. Includes experiments, bean recipes, and
games.
    1. Beans—Juvenile literature. [1. Beans]
I. Silverstein, Virginia B., joint author. II. Title.
SB327.S54   641.3'5'65   74–7311
ISBN 0–13–072637–0

for David Cole

TABLE OF CONTENTS

BEANS

Once upon a time, in Hungary, a poor young man who did not have a job was walking down the road. Suddenly he spied a bean. If I plant this bean, he thought, it will grow into a fine tall bean plant, laden with pods. If I plant the seeds of those bean pods, I'll have dozens, perhaps hundreds of bean plants. If I plant their seeds, soon I'll have enough beans to sell to everyone in the kingdom. I'll be rich! So, placing the bean in his pocket, he raced down the road to the palace and demanded to see the king. He asked the king for barrels and loading places for his coming crops. The king did not realize the young man as yet owned only one bean—he thought he was rich. In fact, so the tale goes, he was so impressed that he offered the young man the hand of his daughter, the princess, in marriage.

Kuan Yu, a great war god in Chinese folktales, was a bean curd seller in his youth. The ancient Romans had a festival on the first of June that they called the Bean Calends, for they offered beans to the dead on that day.

Beans are one of the oldest food plants grown by man, and they are found all over the world. Yet in recent years beans have been making headlines, and they are growing more important all the time. In the United States, soybeans are a multi-billion-dollar-a-year crop. Other countries are so eager to buy our soybean exports that it is hoped that soybeans will be a major help in maintaining a favorable balance of payments for the United States in world trade. Soybeans and other

beans are helping to feed the hungry around the world and offer one of the best hopes for solving food supply problems in the future. For beans are among the most nutritious of all plants, high in a number of important food substances, especially protein, which people need for growth and good health.

There are hundreds of different kinds of beans, which come in a great variety of sizes, shapes, and colors. All of them belong to a larger group of plants called the legume family. The name of the family means "pod"; all the members of the family bear their seeds in the typical long, two-halved pods. Many familiar plants belong to the

3

legume family: not only beans, but also peas, clover, peanuts, licorice, decorative plants such as wisteria and broom, and even trees such as locust, laburnum, and mimosa.

When was the last time you had beans to eat? You may not realize it, but you probably eat and use beans and bean products all through the day, every day of the year. Soybean flour is added to a wide variety of food products, from cereals to sausages. Bean products are used in industry in products from explosives to crayons. The paper this book is printed on and the ink that was used to print it may contain bean products, and the chair you are sitting on may have been glued together with a glue made from beans.

Let's find out more about this interesting and unusual plant.

THE STORY
OF BEANS

Once, long ago, men ate only meat. One day two hunters went out to stalk game. They soon brought down a deer. At noontime, they sat in a forest clearing roasting a haunch of venison. Suddenly a warm wind from the southwest carried a cloud floating right down beside them. A beautiful young woman stepped out of the cloud. "You must be hungry after your long journey, Sky-maiden," said the hunters. "We will share our meal with you." As they ate, the Sky-maiden asked the hunters why they ate only meat. "We have nothing else," they explained. "Return to this clearing tomorrow," said the maiden. "I will repay you for your kindness to me by giving you food for yourselves and for all men hereafter." Then she sailed off in her cloud to the southwest. At sunrise the next morning, when the hunters returned to the clearing, they found that the Skymaiden had kept her promise. From the spot where the maiden's right foot had rested, there had grown a tall corn plant with ripened ears. Curled about it was a vine, laden with bean pods, its roots where her left foot had been.

THE HISTORY OF BEANS

This story was told, in many variations, among the tribes of North American Indians. In some respects it may be quite close to the truth. The first men probably lived by hunting, adding to their meat diet by gathering wild fruits and vegetables that grew in the lands through which they wandered. Gradually groups of men began to settle down. They learned to plant seeds of the best of the wild food plants and care for them while they grew. Legumes were probably among the first of the cultivated plants.

Remains of peas and lentils dating back to about 5500 B.C. have been found in Turkey, and remains of these legumes found in Turkestan are believed to be even older—perhaps as much as a thousand years older. Remains of kidney beans found in caves in Mexico have been dated at about 4000 B.C. So it is known that men were already raising legume crops back in the stone age, before the beginning of written history.

A number of different types of beans grow in different parts of the world. The bean that was common in Europe and the Middle East was the broad bean, *Vicia faba*. It is believed that it originated in Africa and was first domesticated in Asia, west of the Himalayan mountains. In the ancient countries of the Mediterranean region, Assyria, Phoenicia, Palestine, and Egypt, broad beans were one of the main foods. They were usually ground into flour for making bread or stewed in pottage, a kind of soup. (The "mess of pottage" for which the Biblical Esau sold his birthright was made from lentils, a legume related to beans.) Broad beans have been found in funeral offerings placed in Egyptian tombs five thousand years ago. But the priests of ancient Egypt were forbidden to eat beans, which their religion considered unclean.

In ancient Greece and Rome, beans were a major part of the diet of the people, and they also played important roles in their daily lives. Both the Greeks and the Romans used beans for voting. In elections a white bean meant a "yes" vote, while a black bean meant "no." At a trial, a white bean was used to indicate that the prisoner was innocent, while a black bean meant guilty. We use the word "blackballing" today to mean voting to exclude someone; probably the word comes from the custom of voting with black and white beans.

The famous mathematician of ancient Greece, Pythagoras, told his followers not to use beans. There is some disagreement about why Pythagoras said this and what he actually meant. Some scholars believe that he was not really talking about *eating* beans at all. Instead, they say, Pythagoras was advising his followers not to meddle in politics, since beans were used for voting in elections. Other scholars believe that Pythagoras shared a belief, common at the time, that beans contain the souls of people who have died. One should not eat beans, or even walk in a bean field, for fear of hurting these souls.

Whatever the cause, Pythagoras's theories about beans brought him to a sad end. He was being pursued by political enemies, it is said, when he came to the edge of a bean field. Rather than enter the field, he stopped and allowed himself to be captured, and his enemies slew him.

In ancient Rome, beans were highly valued. One of the great families of Rome, the family of Fabius, was proud to take its name from *faba*, the Latin word for bean, in honor of their ancestors, who had grown fields of beans. Roman women smeared a paste made from bean flour on their skin—they thought it was good for removing wrinkles. Bruised beans boiled with garlic were considered a good cough remedy in ancient times.

At least two centuries before Christ, the Romans knew that beans and other legume crops could help enrich the soil. They practiced a form of crop rotation, planting grain crops in a field one year and legume crops the next. We know now that the legumes replace nitrogen substances that grain crops take out of the soil.

The Romans carried beans to the countries they conquered. Gradually broad beans spread through Europe, and soon they were established in England as well. The name of the vegetable changed from the Latin *faba*, first to *haba*, then to *bana*, and finally to *bean* or *bene*.

The common beans of the Americas, *Phaseolus vulgaris*, are believed to have originated in Central America. Gradually they spread north and south, and became an important part of the Indians' diet. Pottery vessels containing dried beans have been found in tombs in the Andes mountains of South America, dating back to before the times of the Incas. In one tomb there were jars decorated with figures of men and women holding beans in one hand and maize in the other. Christopher Columbus and other explorers found Indians raising various types of beans and brought samples back to Europe with them. It was quickly discovered that dried beans are a convenient and nourishing food to carry on sea voyages. Beans became a standard item of supply for seafaring explorers, who helped spread them to other countries. Soon the American green beans were being widely grown in various countries of Europe, where they were known as haricot beans, kidney beans, or Indian beans. (In England, they were sometimes referred to as "French beans," because they became established in France earlier than in England.)

The European settlers of North America quickly learned from the Indians how to grow and prepare the native vegetables, and beans were an important part of their diet. The Pilgrims' first Thanksgiving dinner certainly included dishes of beans, and beans helped to keep them alive all year round. As they had learned from the Indians, the Pilgrims grew beans between the rows of corn. The bean vines twined up around the cornstalks to reach the sunlight. The Indians also taught the Pilgrims how to bake beans.

Navy beans (dried, mature seeds of a variety of the common bean) were first soaked to make them swell and soften their skins. Then they were baked overnight with deer fat and an onion in a clay pot, placed in a hole in the ground lined with hot stones.

The Pilgrims were very serious about their religion, and one of their religious laws forbade the women to cook on Sundays. Baked beans were a perfect dish for Sunday dinner, since they could be prepared the night before. Later, baked beans became a traditional meal for Saturday night supper. The people of Boston made baked beans a specialty, substituting pork for the deer fat and adding brown sugar and various seasonings. For many years, baked beans were baked by bakers. Each family had its own bean pot, which the baker would pick up on Saturday morning. He took the pot to a community oven and returned the pot of baked beans at night, along with hot, fresh brown bread. Boston became so famous for its baked beans that the city gained the nickname of "Beantown."

Modern varieties of *Phaseolus* are still the most widely eaten beans in the Western Hemisphere, and in many parts of Europe as well. But the number one bean crop grown in the United States today is not a common bean variety at all; it is not even a native American bean. It is the soybean, *Glycine max.*

Soybeans are native to eastern Asia. The oldest written records of them date back to 2838 B.C., when the Emperor Shung Nung of China wrote a description of the plant. The ancient Chinese considered soybeans to be their most important crop, and one of the five sacred grains necessary for living. (The other four were rice, wheat, barley, and millet.) They developed methods of producing various types of food from soybeans: a kind of soybean "milk," which was used either fresh or in the production of a vegetable cheese called tofu; a protein-rich film called yuba (produced on the surface of soybean milk when it is boiled); sauces; and soybean paste. They sprouted the soybean seeds and ate the bean sprouts as a vegetable. Around the fourth century A.D., methods were developed for pressing soybean oil from the seeds. Meanwhile, the cultivation of soybeans had spread to Japan and other countries of East Asia, where the beans were prepared in similar ways.

Europeans did not learn about soybeans until a German botanist, Engelbert Kaempfer, spent three years in Japan (from 1690 to 1693). Kaempfer brought some soybeans back to Europe with him, and during the seventeenth century they were grown as a curiosity in a number of European botanical gardens. Soybeans were first carried to the United States around 1800, when a ship brought some to Philadelphia. Commodore Perry brought back a few varieties from his expedition to Japan in 1854. But it was a long time before soybean cultivation really became established outside the Orient, mainly because soybeans cannot be prepared and eaten in the same ways as the native European and American legumes.

As soybean varieties were brought to the United States, the Department of Agriculture gradually tested about 10,000 different kinds. New varieties with higher yield and oil content and more convenient growth habits were developed. Now soybeans are the number one cash crop in the United States, representing more than three-quarters of the world's soybean supply. Soybeans are used not only as foods for humans (in the form of flour, oils, sauces, milk substitutes, and meat substitutes and "extenders") and animal feeds, but also in the production of more than 250 industrial products, including paints, adhesives, soaps, lubricants, and fertilizer.

BEANS IN LEGEND
AND LORE

Beans are such an important food all over the world, that it is not surprising that they have found their way into many common figures of speech. "Full of beans" means full of health and high spirits (or in another variation, full of "hot air"). In some sayings, such as "I haven't a bean," "beans" are used as a synonym for money or property. It is believed that such phrases come from a confusion with an old French word, *biens*, which means "property." But phrases like "not worth a bean" or "doesn't amount to a hill of beans," refer to the bean's small value.

The phrase "he doesn't know beans," meaning that he doesn't know very much, may refer to an old riddle:

Q. How many beans make five?
A. Five beans, of course.
   Everybody knows that.
Q. But you don't know how many
   blue beans make five
   white ones.
A. Five—if peeled.

Probably one of the first fairytales you ever heard was "Jack and the Beanstalk." This same theme, in numerous variations, is found among peoples all over the world, from Icelanders to Zulus. The beanstalk in such tales is a symbol for a ladder or road to the heavens. In the version most familiar to us, which originated as an old German tale, Jack is a symbol for man, who takes and uses the treasures of the supreme being. When he climbs the beanstalk to the land in the clouds, he steals three treasures of the giant (the All-Father): a bag of riches (rain), a hen that lays the golden egg (sun), and a magic harp (wind maker). In another version of the tale, told in New Guinea, a man and his mother climb the beanstalk to kill Tauni-kapi-kapi, a man-eating giant (storms).

The bean played an important role in traditional Twelfth Night celebrations in England. Raisin cakes were baked and given to the guests. One of them also contained a bean. The man who received the bean was the Bean King, who would reign over the festivities. In early times he reigned through the whole twelve days from Christmas to Twelfth Night, and he performed certain magic duties to ensure good weather for the coming year. As these pagan practices were dropped, the Bean King came to be crowned on the Twelfth Night. In another variation, a bean was placed in one cake and a pea in another. The man who found the bean was the king, and the girl who found the pea was his queen.

American Indian tribes told how the Skymaiden first gave beans and corn to men. Others said that these gifts were brought by a black crow, who carried a corn grain in one ear and a bean in the other. They explained their practice of growing corn and beans together by a beautiful legend.

The cornstalk was a tall young man, who sang of his loneliness and his wish for a wife. The first to answer him was the pumpkin maiden, with her trailing vine and yellow flowers. But the pumpkin maiden wandered over the ground so much that the cornstalk could not go with her. So she trailed away, weeping. Then the slender bean vine came. She twined her tendrils around the cornstalk and promised to love him forever. And ever since, the bean twines about the corn, and he supports her with his sturdy stalk.

Peoples in different parts of the world do not agree about whether beans are a symbol of good or bad. In China beans were a good-luck symbol. A person who wore a string of soybeans hidden around his neck was believed to possess magic powers to do amazing feats. Three dark soybeans soaked in sesame oil for three days were used to foretell the future.

Folk medicine also had an important place for beans. One obvious use was suggested by their shape. Since beans look like little kidneys, they must be good for treating kidney problems. So beans were recommended as a diuretic, to help the kidneys eliminate excess water from the body. Bean pods steeped in wine or vinegar and the distilled juice of the flowers were thought to improve the complexion; a lotion made from bean meal mixed with cold milk was also recommended. Poultices made from bean flowers, leaves, and bean meal were used to reduce inflammation and swelling. Perhaps there may be some benefit in some of these bean prescriptions; modern medical researchers occasionally discover a new and effective drug by the study of old folk remedies made from plants. But one of the most spectacular successes of bean remedies probably has a different explanation. It is said that warts can be cured by rubbing them with the white inner lining of a bean pod, then throwing the pod away or burying it in a secret place. As the pod rots, the warts disappear. This charm often seems to work. But doctors studying warts have made some important discoveries in recent years. First of all, warts are apparently caused by a virus. And, surprisingly, a strong suggestion—such as when the person is hypnotized or believes in the power of a charm—can make warts go away, just as mysteriously as they appeared.

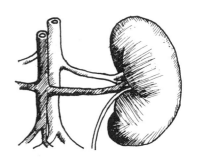

THE LIFE STORY
OF THE BEAN

A bean, like all flowering plants, starts its life as a seed. It is a rather large seed, with plenty of stored food to be used by the new plant-to-be.

THE BEAN SEED

If you look at a bean seed, you will notice first a sort of scar on one side. This scar is called the *hilum*, and it marks the place where the bean seed was attached in the bean pod. Looking more closely, you will notice a tiny hole at one end of the hilum. This hole is called the *micropyle*, and it has two important parts to play in the life of a bean.

The bean seed is wrapped in a tough, protective seed coat. If you were to carefully

18

slit the seed coat the long way around the bean, from one end of the hilum to the other, you would find that the bean seed inside contains two fleshy halves. These are the *cotyledons*, in which food for the young growing plant is stored. Plants store food mainly in the form of starch. You can see this for yourself with a simple test. Lightly brush some tincture of iodine along the cotyledon. Iodine reacts with starch to give a purple color.

Parting the two cotyledons carefully, you will find, nestled between them, the tiny embryo. This is like a plant in miniature. It has two tiny leaves (the *plumule*) and a little root (the *radicle*). The stemlike middle part connecting them is called the *hypocotyl*. These are the parts that can grow into a bean plant. But they could not get started without the stored food in the cotyledons.

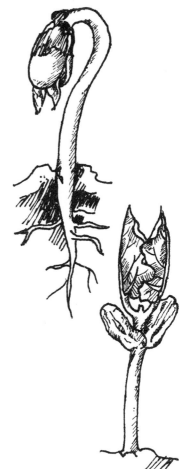

HOW THE BEAN GROWS

When a bean seed is planted, it sprouts or *germinates*. The embryo root pokes its tip out through the micropyle and grows out into the soil. Tiny root hairs form along the growing root. They take in moisture and dissolved minerals from the soil.

Meanwhile, the hypocotyl is getting

19

longer. Suddenly it pushes up out of the soil —the first part of the seedling to emerge. It is bent over, for the cotyledons are still buried in the soil. So the bean seedling looks at first like the top of a hairpin.

The hypocotyl continues to grow and begins to straighten up. It pulls on the cotyledons and plumule. Within a day or so, the seed coat splits, and the top of the plant pops up out of the soil. The empty seed coat is left behind, buried beneath the surface.

Now the young bean seedling is growing straight upward. At the top, the two seed leaves unfold and grow quickly. Farther down the stem are the two cotyledons. As sun shines on the growing bean plant, the leaves, cotyledon, and stem soon turn green. This marks the beginning of a turning point in the life of the plant.

A growing plant, like a growing child, needs food: food for energy and food for building materials. The sprouting bean embryo takes the food it needs from the reserves stored in the cotyledons. Even after it has burst out of the soil and become a green seedling, for a time it continues to draw upon the food reserves in the cotyledons. But there is a limit to the amount of food the mother plant stored in the cotyledons. Gradually they shrivel, and at last fall off. Now the young bean plant is on its own. But it still needs a constant supply of food.

FOOD FOR THE
BEAN PLANT

New food for the growing bean plant is manufactured in the leaves. Their green color is due to the presence of a green pigment called *chlorophyll*. Chlorophyll in plants acts as a sort of energy trap. When sunlight shines on a plant, the chlorophyll in its leaves and stem holds some of the sunlight energy and helps change it into a form that can power chemical reactions.

The surface of a plant leaf looks solid. But under a magnifier it can be seen that it contains many tiny openings, called *stomates*. Each of these tiny openings is guarded by a pair of bean-shaped cells called *guard cells*. The guard cells can swell to close the stomates or shrink to open them. Usually the stomates are open during the day and nearly closed at night. When the stomates are open, gases from the air pass freely in and out. Air is a mixture of gases: about four-fifths nitrogen, about one-fifth oxygen (the gas we need to breathe), and smaller amounts of carbon dioxide, water vapors, and other gases. Carbon dioxide and water are the main building blocks that plants use to make their food. They get carbon dioxide from the air and water both from the air and, even more, from the soil, through the roots. In the plant leaves, carbon dioxide and water are combined, using the sunlight energy trapped by chlorophyll, into sugars, starches, and other complicated chemicals. Scientists call this process *photosynthesis* (photo means light, and synthesis means a putting together). Oxygen is produced as a by-product of photosynthesis and passes out into the air through the stomates.

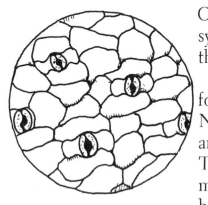

Using the food that it is now making for itself, the bean plant continues to grow. New leaves form at the tip of the stem. They are different from the first two seed leaves. The new leaves are compound leaves, each made up of three leaflets. Now the adult bean plant starts to take shape. Bush beans are short, bushy plants, with many leaves branching out from the central stem, close together. Pole beans are long and slender plants. If there is nothing to support them, they will grow out flat along the ground. But if there is a convenient pole or trellis or cornstalk, the bean plants will climb it.

UNDERGROUND ACTIVITY

While the part of the bean plant above the ground is growing vigorously, putting out new leaves, and producing food, the roots, buried in the soil, are also doing their share. Water and dissolved minerals are absorbed from the soil through the delicate root hairs and are then carried up through all parts of the plant along thin conducting tubes that run through the roots, stems, and leaves. (The veins that can be seen branching out through the leaf are part of this plant conducting system.)

Meanwhile small knoblike growths have formed on the roots. These structures are called *nodules*, and they are filled with bacteria. The bacteria that live in the nodules of beans and other legumes are not disease germs. They work in partnership with the plants, receiving shelter and food substances from the plants and in turn providing the plants with a substance they can use: ammonia. Ammonia is a chemical compound in which nitrogen is combined with hydrogen. Plants, like animals, need nitrogen to build proteins. Some proteins are building materials, which help to give living things shape and form. Others are enzymes, chemicals that help other chemicals to react. Nitrogen is also a part of the nucleic acids, the chemicals of heredity that carry the blueprints of how an organism will develop and help to regulate all the chemical processes that go on inside it through its entire life.

The air that passes in through a plant's stomata is about four-fifths nitrogen. But this nitrogen gas is not a form that plants can use. They can use only nitrogen that is combined with other substances in compounds such as ammonia, nitrites, and nitrates. Animals cannot use nitrogen gas, either. They must take in various nitrogen compounds with their food. But certain kinds of bacteria do have the ability to bind or fix the nitrogen from the atmosphere in chemical compounds. Some of these *nitrogen-fixing bacteria* live in the soil. Others are found in the soil but cannot fix nitrogen unless they are able to invade the roots of legumes. They stimulate the cells of the roots to divide and form nodules. There the bacteria live, using the sugars that the plant provides to produce ammonia—far more than they need for themselves. The legume plant benefits from the extra ammonia produced by its bacteria "guests," and part of it passes out into the soil, where it may aid the growth of nearby plants. Farmers have found that beans and other legumes are a sort of "green fertilizer," which leave the soil they grow in richer than they found it. Legume crops may be planted side by side with other plants. Or a field may be planted with legumes one year and with other crops the next. Sometimes farmers plant a legume crop such as alfalfa or vetch and then plow the whole plants under, to help enrich the soil for future crops.

THE BEAN FLOWER

When a bean plant has been growing strongly and vigorously for a time, small stems begin to sprout from the angles between the leaf stalks and the main stem. These new stems bear groups of flowers.

Most bean plants belong to the group called annuals. They live for just a single growing season, and then they wither and die. The flower is the bean's way of providing for the next generation, so that there can be new bean plants the following year.

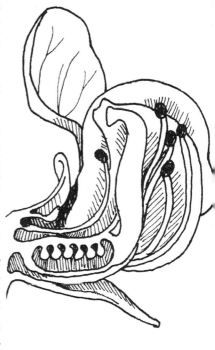

The flowers of bean plants have the same basic parts as most other flowers. Growing out from the flower stalk is a green cup called the *calyx*, shaped like a five-pointed star. Each leaflike "arm" of the star is called a *sepal*. Within the cup of sepals is a ring of five *petals*. The petals of some flowers are all alike and are arranged in a circle or a series of circles. But the bean flower has three different kinds of petals. At the top is the largest petal, called the banner or standard. Before the flower is fully opened, the standard is often folded protectively over the other petals. Later it stands up straight like the banner for which it is named. Below the banner, extended like the wings of a butterfly, are two narrower petals, called wings. Between the wings is another pair of petals, joined at their lower edges to form a shape like the keel of a boat. This is the keel. Depending on the type of bean, the flowers may be white, yellowish, or purplish.

Within the keel are the most important parts of the flower—the male and female organs that contain the special reproductive cells that can start a new life. There are ten male organs, called *stamens*. Each one consists of a head, called an *anther*, mounted on a stalk called a *filament*. In bean flowers, nine of the stamens are fused together into a sort of tube, while the tenth stamen stands alone. Within the tube formed by the stamens is the female organ of the flower: the *pistil*. The pistil of a flower is usually shaped like a vase, with a swollen base (the *ovary*), a slender neck (the *style*), and an enlarged top portion called the *stigma*.

Powdery grains of *pollen*, which contain the male cells, are produced in the anther. *Ovules*, the eggs that can develop into seeds, are enclosed within the ovary. Pollen and ovules must be brought together to form a seed.

POLLINATION

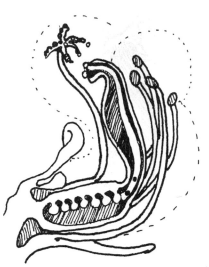

Since each bean flower contains both stamens and pistil, it can be self-pollinated, with pollen from the anthers being transferred to the stigma of the same flower. But sometimes bean flowers are cross-pollinated by insect visitors, such as honeybees.

As a bee buzzes through the air, it is attracted by the showy petals of flowers and by their fragrance. It alights to pick up a load of pollen and nectar (a sweet, sugary liquid) to carry home to the hive. But in doing so, without intending to, it helps the flower as well.

When a bee alights on a bean flower, it reaches out with its *proboscis*, a kind of sucking tube, to sip up the nectar. But the bean flower is built in such a way that its proboscis first touches the stigma, the sticky top part of the pistil, and leaves a load of pollen that it has picked up from other bean flowers. Then the bee's proboscis touches the style of the flower. In bean flowers, the style is coil-shaped and covered with a brush of tiny hairs. Powdery pollen that sprinkles down from the anthers tends to collect on this brush. When the bee touches it with its proboscis, it picks up a new load of pollen,

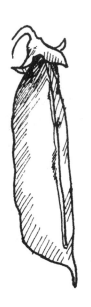

which it and may leave on the stigma of the next bean flower it visits.

FROM FLOWER TO SEED

When a pollen grain is deposited on the stigma, it begins to germinate. A tiny tube, so small that it could not be seen without a microscope, grows down the style into the ovary, curves around under one of the ovules, and grows in through its micropyle. (The micropyle thus serves both as an entranceway for the pollen tube into the ovule and an exit opening for the embryo root of the germinating seed.) The sperms, the male cells of the plant, travel down the pollen tube and into the ovule. Now the seed is fertilized, and the embryo and cotyledons begin to develop. One pollen grain is needed to fertilize each ovule in the ovary.

After the ovules have been fertilized, the ovary of the flower begins to grow into the typical legume pod. The petals shrivel and fall off, but if you look at a bean pod you can clearly see the sepals at the base of the pod and the shriveled remains of the stigma and style at its tip. Botanists, people who study plants, call the structure that grows from the ovary of a flowering plant and encloses its seeds a fruit. The bean pod thus is really a fruit, even though people usually regard it as a vegetable.

If the pods of the common bean of the Americas are picked while they are still green and fleshy, they are good food for humans. In this form they are called snap beans (because they make a snapping sound if they are broken crosswise), green beans, or string beans. (The bean pods of the original varieties contained tough fibers, which ran lengthwise down the seams of the pod and had to be removed before the pods could be sliced. Agricultural researchers have since bred new, "stringless" varieties, so the string bean's name no longer really suits it.)

If the bean pods are left on the plant, they gradually become dry and papery. Then they split open along the edges into two halves or *valves*. The seeds are released, and may fall to the ground, where they may sprout and grow into new bean plants. Pods that open to release their seeds are called *dehiscent* pods.

The dry, hard seeds of ripe bean pods are harvested and eaten in numerous ways. Depending on the variety of bean, these seeds vary in color and shape, and are sold under such names as navy beans, pinto beans, and kidney beans.

KINDS OF BEANS

What do castor beans, coffee beans, and Mexican jumping beans have in common? Not very much, really. For in spite of their names and their beanlike shape, these seeds are borne by plants that do not belong to the legume family.

THE LEGUME FAMILY

The "real" beans are all legumes, plants that bear their seeds in long pods that split into two valves. Their roots form nodules, in which nitrogen-fixing bacteria live.

The names that people commonly give to plants and animals are often confusing. For example, cowpeas and chick peas are really beans, while some "beans" are not beans at all. Scientists, who must know exactly what organisms they are dealing with, have worked out a system of classifying the creatures of our world according to their similarities and differences. Each separate kind of animal or plant is given a two-part name, which is usually made up of Latin or Greek words. The first part of the name refers to a grouping called a *genus*, which includes a number of *species* or separate types of plants or animals that are very similar and seem to be closely related. The second part of the name refers to the species. Usually the names are selected to describe various characteristics of the organism. For instance, the scientific name for human beings is *Homo sapiens: Homo* means "man," while *sapiens* means "thinking." Sometimes it is necessary to divide a species into still smaller groups, called *varieties*. This happens especially often with cultivated plants, for people have taken the original species and, over many generations, bred them into a great variety of forms.

Genera (the plural of genus) are grouped into larger subdivisions, called *families*, which in turn are grouped with related families into still larger subdivisions, and so on up the line. Thus, each kind of plant or animal has its own place in the family tree of life.

Beans belong to the *kingdom* of plants, and within this kingdom to the division or *phylum* of *tracheophytes*—plants

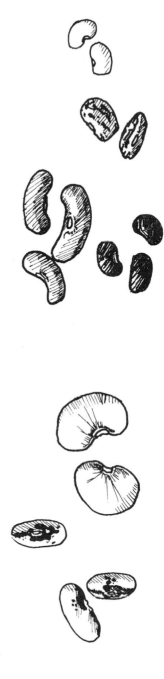

with tubelike conducting vessels through which water and other substances are carried through the plant. Within the phylum, beans belong to the *class* of *angiosperms*, the flowering plants, and within that to the *subclass* of *dicots*—plants whose seeds have two cotyledons. Notice that as we go down the line we find out more and more information about the special characteristics of a plant. Within the legume family, beans (together with peas and some other legumes) are usually placed in a subfamily called *Papilionoideae*. This name comes from a word meaning "butterfly." It refers to the shape of the pea and bean flowers, which look somewhat like a butterfly.

AMERICAN BEANS

Many of the American beans belong to the genus *Phaseolus*. Hundreds of varieties of the common bean, *Phaseolus vulgaris*, are cultivated. The fleshy young pods of this species are eaten as snap beans or string beans. Varieties with yellow pods are usually called wax beans or butter beans. The white navy beans, red beans, pink beans, spotted pinto beans, and the large red kidney-shaped kidney beans are all seeds of *Phaseolus vulgaris* varieties. So are the black beans that are called frijoles in Mexico. The variety that produces kidney beans grows in low bushes, while navy beans grow on a vine-type plant.

Lima beans belong to the species *Phaseolus limensis*. The broad, flat pods of this plant are not edible, even when they are young. The ripe pods split open and curl to release the seeds, which are large, white or pale green, and flattened. Lima beans are perennial plants in the tropics, living on from one year to the next. But they are usually cultivated as annuals, plowing under the old plants and replanting new ones each year. They need a longer growing season and warmer weather than most varieties of the common bean. Like the common beans, lima beans grow in both bush and climbing varieties. Their small, greenish-white flowers grow in clusters, like fleecy white plumes.

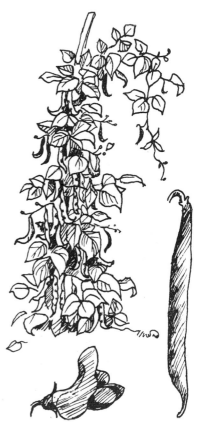

The tepary, *Phaseolus acutifolius*, thrives in dry desert regions. It is grown in Mexico and the southwestern United States for its small, variously colored seeds. Ripe tepary beans may be yellow, tawny, brown, red, blue-black, white, or speckled. This was the favorite bean of the southwestern Indians.

The scarlet runner bean, *Phaseolus multiflorus*, was originally an American bean, but now it is grown even more widely in Europe. This is a fast-growing plant, with large, bright red flowers. In the United States it is grown mainly as an ornamental plant, but in Europe its seeds, speckled with red-and-black spots, and its pods are eaten. This is one of the beans that grows wild as a perennial, but is usually cultivated as an annual.

BEANS OF EUROPE AND ASIA

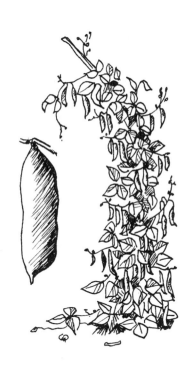

The mung bean, *Phaseolus aureus*, is important in Asia. Its slender, three- or four-inch pods contain about a dozen tiny seeds, only an eighth of an inch in diameter. The seeds are sprouted, and the shoots are either cooked as a vegetable or eaten raw in salads.

The original Old World bean, *Vicia faba*, has been replaced to a great degree by *Phaseolus* varieties. But it is still grown, especially in England, where it is called the Windsor bean or broad bean. Another name for this bean is the horse bean; it makes a good fodder crop for animals. This bean needs cooler growing weather than the American beans, and it does not do well in the high summer temperatures. It has large, white flowers, marked with purplish blue, which would seem to be well suited to attracting insects. But it has been found that these flowers are nearly always self-pollinated.

Chick peas or garbanzo beans (*Cicer*

arietinum) are large, pea-shaped seeds with a nut flavor. They were cultivated in the ancient lands of the eastern Mediterranean region and later spread to India and other parts of Asia. The family of the ancient Roman statesman Cicero got its name from this bean. Chick peas, called ceci in Italy, are cooked as a vegetable or pickled in vinegar and oil for salads.

The cowpea, *Vigna sinensis*, is an ancient bean species, native to India. In Asia it is an important food plant, and it is also grown in the southern United States. Here it is usually called the black-eye pea or black-eye bean, because of the characteristic black ring around the hilum of the seed.

Still another Asian import, the guar bean (*Cyamopsis tetragonoloba*), is a native of India, where it has been used for centuries as a food and forage crop. The tiny guar beans (less than a quarter of an inch in diameter) are grown in the United States mainly for the guar gum that is produced from them. This substance is used in industry as a settling agent, a water sealer, a suspending agent, and a stabilizer in such varied products as explosives, ceramics, crayons, detergents, inks, textiles, ice cream, sausages, cheese spreads, and cosmetics. A by-product, guar meal, is used as a protein supplement in livestock feeds.

THE SOYBEAN– NUMBER ONE

The beans mentioned in this chapter so far are important food crops for humans and animals and are also grown widely for soil improvement and industrial uses. But all of them put together probably would not equal the annual crop of another kind of bean, the soybean *(Glycine max)*. In 1970, according to U.S. government statistics, while less than two million acres were planted to green beans, with a value of about $250 million, more than 40 million acres were planted to soybeans, with a value of about $2.5 billion. The United States produces more than three-quarters of the world supply of soybeans, and exports more than half of its crop.

What is there about soybeans to make them the nation's number one cash crop? Soybeans might well claim to be an "everything plant." Soybeans are rich in protein and oil. Indeed, soybeans are one of the most efficient sources of protein known to man. An acre of grazing land will yield 43 pounds of beef cattle protein, while the same area planted in soybeans will yield 600 pounds of soybean protein. Unlike the proteins of most other plants, soybeans contain all the amino acids needed by humans and thus make an ideal "meat extender" and meat substitute. Soybeans have more protein than beef, more calcium than milk, and more of a fatty substance called lecithin than eggs. They are rich in vitamins and minerals.

When soybeans were first grown in the United States, the plants were usually mowed as hay and used as feed for livestock. Soybeans are still used in this way, and also as a "green manure" crop for enriching soil. But more often the plants are grown for the beans, which are crushed and separated into soybean oil (about one-fifth of the bean) and flakes that are processed into soybean meal. Most of the meal produced is still used as livestock feed, providing more than half of all the protein meal fed to hogs, chickens, cattle, and other farm animals. Some of the meal is ground into soy flour, used in such foods as soups, puddings, breads, cereals, and macaroni products. (Whenever you see "protein-enriched flour" on a label, it is probably soybean.) Methods have been devised to give soy protein a fiberlike texture, and it is used as an extender in meat products from franks to hamburgers and even to produce artificial "chicken," "bacon," and "cheese." Soybean oil is used in cooking and salad oils, margarines, and shortenings. Soybean oil and meal are also used in such varied industrial products as paint, waterproof ce-

ment, ink, soap, linoleum backing, insect sprays, synthetic rubber, plastics, drugs, and cosmetics.

Soybeans grow on a bushy plant, about three feet high. Like the common beans, the leaves (except for the two first leaves) grow in groups of three leaflets. The stem, leaves, and pods are covered with short, fine brown or gray hairs. The well-branched roots grow as deep as four or five feet, which helps to give the soybean a great resistance to drought. Small white or purple flowers appear where the leaf joins the stem. They are usually self-pollinated and grow into pods holding two or three seeds. Soybean pods vary in color from light yellow to green, brown, black, or speckled. Wild soybean pods open as they ripen and scatter their seeds readily. But most commercial varieties have been specially selected for the ability to hold their seeds for two weeks or more after maturity. (This makes them much easier to harvest with machines.) Usually the soybean leaves turn yellow and drop off as the pods ripen, so the plant just before harvesting presents a rather scraggly appearance.

The soybeans themselves are about the size of peas and may be yellow, green, brown, or black. Some green or yellow seeds have a saddle-like patch of black or brown extending down on each side of the hilum.

Soybeans have a strong, bitter-bean taste that most people find unpleasant. But modern methods of processing, particularly the removal of carbohydrates (sugars and starches), have helped to solve the problem. These methods have also helped to solve another problem that many people have with beans: these vegetables tend to produce a great deal of gas in the intestines, which can cause both pain and embarrassment. Beans have long had the reputation of being "gassy" foods. As an irreverent jingle proclaims:

Beans, beans, the musical fruit,
The more you eat, the more you toot.

BEANS IN THE GARDEN AND MARKETPLACE

Beans are a favorite vegetable among home gardeners. They are hardy and productive plants. Bush beans are particularly easy to grow, and they are ready for the table only 50 days after planting. Pole beans usually take a little longer.

BEANS FOR THE HOME GARDEN

The best time to plant beans varies from place to place, depending on the climate. Generally, the first beans should be planted in the spring, as soon as the danger of frost has passed and the soil has warmed up to about 65°. (Beans planted in soil that is too cold germinate very slowly, if at all, and the cotyledons rot in the ground before the growing seedling can pull them out.)

Beans are planted one to two inches deep, in rich, loose, well-drained soil. Be sure to plant the seeds deep enough; if they are too close to the surface, the root might poke up out of the soil and then dry out before it can turn downward.

Bush beans are usually planted in rows two to three feet apart, with the plants spaced about two to four inches apart in each row. Pole beans are usually planted in groups of from four to six seeds, called "hills." (That is the "hill of beans" in the old saying.) Why so many seeds together? Perhaps the answer lies in the old English rhyme:

One to rot and one to grow,
One for pigeon, one for the crow.

In addition to pigeons and crows, the home gardener must also contend with various caterpillars, beetles, aphids, leaf hoppers, slugs, and other pests. If you spot a caterpillar on a bean plant, pick it off and dispose of it immediately. (Often caterpillars are active at night and spend the day resting in the soil near the base of the plant.) Snails and slugs are attracted by baits, such as a low dish filled with stale beer. (They seem to find beer so irresistible that they crawl right into it and drown.) Various pesticide sprays and dusts are available for controlling insect pests and diseases of bean plants. But they should be used sparingly and with great caution, exactly according to the directions on the label. (Some of them are poisonous to people as

well as insect pests.) Gardeners and farmers in rural areas must also worry about woodchucks, which find the tender hypocotyls of young bean sprouts especially tasty. A sturdy fence, with the bottom buried in the soil, is usually the best protection against these furry pests.

Bush beans are bushy, low-growing plants, which yield a large crop for the amount of space they take up. Pole beans need a more elaborate setup: a support on which they can twine. If poles are used, the bean plants take better to slightly rough poles, such as a trimmed tree branch, rather than smooth poles. (Their tendrils can get a firmer grip on the rough surfaces.) Instead of a single pole, you can use three poles, set in a triangle at the base, with the tops bound together like the framework of an Indian tepee. Pole beans will also climb a trellis or a fence.

When to pick the beans depends on your taste. Some people think they taste best when they are only about two inches long and especially young and tender. Others prefer to wait until the pods have reached their full size. But at any rate, green beans should be picked while they still make a sharp snapping sound when they are broken. If they are left until they become overripe, the pods grow tough and then papery. (Beans grown for seeds are picked at the papery stage.)

It might seem tempting to use dried beans from the grocery store to plant for the home garden. They are much cheaper than beans sold especially for planting. But this is not usually a good idea. First of all, commercial bean varieties are very specialized. The beans grown for seeds usually have tough, stringy, unappetizing pods, which are not at all good for eating as snap beans. (The commercial snap beans, on the other hand, usually are not very good seed producers.) In addition, the seeds sold for planting are often specially selected for high resistance to disease and adapted to the conditions of the home garden.

BEANS FOR THE MARKETPLACE

Though beans are a favorite crop of home gardeners all over the world, today most beans are grown on large farms. Modern farming is big business. Machines are used for tilling the soil, planting, applying fertilizer, weeding, spraying pesticides, and harvesting.

Beans grown commercially are usually planted in rows, in well-drained soil. Like garden beans, they are planted when the soil has warmed in the spring, after the danger of frost is over.

A number of diseases such as blight, rust, mildew, and mosaic may plague bean crops. They cause spots and pits on the leaves, stems, and pods, and the pods and seeds may develop poorly. These diseases are generally caused by fungi and viruses, which may be spread by insects such as aphids and leaf hoppers. Mexican beetles devour the soft parts of bean leaves, leaving bare skeletons. Pesticides can help keep these and other pests under control. But the best protection against fungus diseases is often prevention, through the use of disease-free seeds and disease-resistant plants. Crop rotation is also a good idea for beans. Fungus spores from infected bean plants may remain in the soil for a year or more, ready to infect a new crop of beans planted in the same soil. Usually bean diseases are harmless to other plants, and those of other plants do not affect beans. Thus, planting a series of crops in a

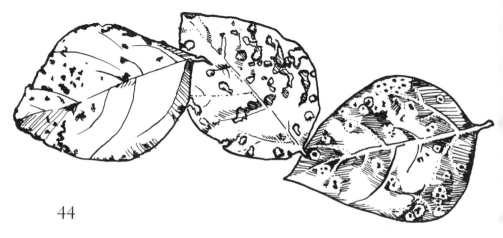

44

field, such as corn, wheat, and a green manure crop before planting beans again can help keep all the crops healthy.

Beans that are grown for edible pods are usually harvested with special machines when the pods are at just the right stage of ripeness. Large producers of canned or frozen beans have a variety of machines for sorting and grading the beans, washing them, snipping off the ends, cooking and cooling them, and packaging them.

Dried beans are usually processed in elevators to clean them, remove small stones, straw, and other foreign materials, and screen them by size. At large processing terminals, electric-eye sorting machines separate the good beans from split or discolored beans. Private, state, or federal inspectors examine bean shipments and grade them according to their quality. Only the good beans are sold as food for humans; split and damaged beans are used for livestock feed.

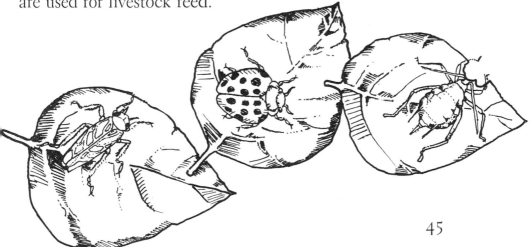

BEANS FOR
THE FUTURE

Have you had any bacon analog for breakfast lately? Tried a miso-and-jelly sandwich? How about a helping of tempeh or sufu? As the years go by, these and other soybean foods will become increasingly familiar to Americans. Rising prices of foods in general and meats in particular have helped to make high-protein foods derived from beans more acceptable to the eating public.

Although soybean meat substitutes are being welcomed by thrifty Americans, much of the research that made them possible was originally aimed at producing better low-cost foods to help feed the hungry millions of the developing nations.

Millions of children in Africa and Latin America suffer from a disease called kwashiorkor. In a dialect spoken in Ghana, "kwashiorkor" means literally, "first-second." It is an illness that the first child gets when a second is born, and the older child no longer receives his mother's milk. Usually some starchy food like cassava or tapioca is substituted. Then, even though the child's belly may be filled, he is no longer getting enough protein. His feet and legs swell and his belly becomes bloated. His skin becomes cracked and pale, and his hair changes to a red or dirty gray color. Unless his diet is improved, he becomes listless and may die. If he survives, his physical and mental growth are often stunted.

One of the problems in trying to help people who are not getting enough of the right kind of foods is that people are often slow to accept changes. They cling to their old food habits and are suspicious of new and different-tasting foods, even when they are suffering from hunger. Soybeans are providing an important ingredient in a number of products that are already helping to ease the problems of world hunger.

One product, CSM, costs less than 8 cents a pound, yet three and a half ounces of it can supply half or more of all the known nutrients and a third of the calories needed by a one- to three-year-old child for one day. CSM is a blend of corn, soybean, and milk products. It can be made into soup, beverages, gruel, bread, or pudding, and thus people can serve it in familiar ways. Billions of pounds of CSM have already been distributed in more than a hundred developing countries and are helping to wipe out kwashiorkor. Newer high-protein food supplements for children include WSB (a wheat-soy blend), a flour made by mixing soy protein with bananas, and a mixture of ground chick peas, sesame flour, and low-fat soybean flour.

Meanwhile, agricultural researchers have been working to improve some soybean foods popular in the Orient. One of these is sufu, a cheese made from the soybean curd, tofu. Sufu made by the centuries-old method often has an unpleasant beany flavor. But now scientists have isolated a fungus that ferments the soybean cheese to produce a soft, pale yellow product with a pleasant taste and aroma. Flavors pleasing to Western tastes can easily be incorporated into the cheese during the last step of the manufacturing process, by adding garlic, wine, or pepper.

Tempeh is another fermented soybean product popular in the Orient. Modern methods, producing the tempeh in perforated cellophane bags instead of the traditional banana leaves, yield a better-tasting product. Agricultural researchers have also discovered that mold used in the fermenting of tempeh produces compounds that stop the growth of some bacteria. This soybean product may actually help to provide resistance to disease together with good nutrition.

Miso is another fermented soybean product, which has the consistency of peanut butter. It has a spicy flavor and can be used as a spread or dip.

One of the most promising areas of soybean research and development is the production of soy-protein fibers. These shiny fibers are spun on standard textile equipment —just like nylon and other textile fibers— and look like long, silky blond hair. During the spinning process, the diameter of the fibers can be varied from a thousandth of an inch to three-hundredths of an inch—from the most delicate fibrils to tough strands. These soy protein fibers can be used to make textured protein products with a "mouth-feel" similar to that of meat. If the fibers are laid down in a random mat, the product will resemble a ham loaf; laying them parallel to one another will make the soybean "meat" more chewy. Putting advances in spun soy protein technology together with advances

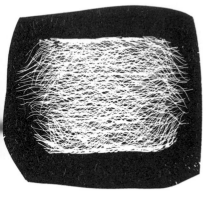

in artificial flavor research, manufacturers can already produce soybean "analogs" of beef, chicken, turkey, bacon, and other meats, which taste and feel just like the real thing.

A soybean bacon analog has much to recommend it over the traditional product. It has only a third of the calories of real bacon and has no cholesterol. It does not shrink during cooking, and it costs only half as much as bacon per serving.

Marketing tests of the bacon analog have already been run, and many consumers were found ready to accept the new product. As might be expected, the bacon analog was especially popular among weight and cholesterol watchers, as well as people interested in "good buys" in food. In future years, this and other soybean products should become familiar items on supermarket shelves.

There is a problem with spun protein meat analogs, however. The spinning process is an expensive one, and many of the analogs are nearly as expensive as the meat they replace. Yet the cheap soy flakes, although 70 percent protein, cannot be molded and made to look like meat.

Another manufacturing process called extruding seems to be solving the problem.

A mixture of soy flour and 30 to 40 percent water is forced through a horizontal cylinder under increasing pressure at temperatures of 300° to 400°F. The combination of heat and pressure breaks down the soybean protein structure, forming a fibrous mass with a consistency like cooked meat. This textured vegetable protein (TVP) is about 50 percent protein and can be used as a meat extender and as imitation tuna and chicken chunks.

In future years, the search for new and better ways to make vegetable proteins tasty and appealing will continue. Soybeans and other members of the bean family will be part of nearly any kind of food products you might want to buy—and probably part of the paper and plastic packages that cover them as well.

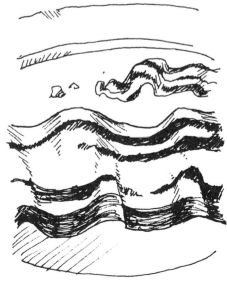

FUN WITH BEANS

EXPERIMENTING WITH BEANS

Beans are among the easiest seeds to grow. Not only is it fun to watch them sprout and grow, but there are many simple experiments you can do with beans, without any need for expensive equipment. In fact, a number of experiments that you can do with beans in your own home or classroom are famous "landmark experiments," by which scientists learned important facts about plants.

Sprouting Beans

Beans can be sprouted either in soil or on a moist blotter. If you sprout beans on a blotter, you can actually watch them at each stage, without having to dig up the germinating seeds to see what is happening. (You can always carefully transfer the seedlings to soil later if you want to continue growing them.)

A good setup to use for watching beans germinate is shown in the picture. All you need is a clean wide-mouth jar (such as a peanut-butter jar), a blotter or folded paper towels, and some water. (And beans, of course! You can use the beans from a seed packet or the dried beans you can buy at the supermarket. You will get faster results if you soak the beans in water for a few hours first.) Roll the blotter or paper towels to form a tube, just wide enough to fit snugly inside the jar. Place the beans around the jar, wedging them between the blotter and the glass walls of the jar, and pour about an inch of water into the bottom of the jar. Water will soak up the blotter and keep the beans moist; add more water when necessary to keep the level up to an inch. (The beans should be above the water level.) It is a good idea to cover the mouth of the jar with a piece of cheesecloth or gauze to keep out dust, for dust particles may carry the spores of fungi that could grow on the beans and kill them.

Why not use the tight-fitting lid that came with the jar? Try a jar that way to see what will happen. (Hint: plants—even seeds—"breathe" just like people do. They take in oxygen from the air and give off carbon dioxide. Will the air inside the jar stay fresh long enough for the beans to sprout?)

When bean seeds germinate in the soil, they are in the dark, where no sunlight can reach them. Will they germinate if they are in the sunlight? Compare three jars of bean seeds: one on the windowsill in direct sunlight, one out in the room, but not in the direct rays of the sun, and one in a dark closet. Which one germinates best?

Which Way is Up?

Does it matter which way you turn a bean seed when you plant it? How does the embryo plant know which way is "up"? Could you ever get a seedling with its roots pointing up in the air and its shoot poking down into the soil? Try arranging a set of bean seeds in different ways: one with its hilum pointing upward, one with the hilum downward, and two others with the hilum pointing to the side (one with the micropyle at the top and the other with the micropyle at the bottom). Which way is the embryo root pointing when it emerges from the micropyle? Which way does it grow? It has been found that no matter which way seeds are pointed when they are planted, they always grow with the shoot upward and the root downward. Scientists call this built-in gravity sense of plants *geotropism* (which comes from words meaning "earth" and "turning").

It is not only sprouting seeds that show geotropism. If you take a seedling that is growing well and turn it on its side, you will soon see its shoot bend upward and its root bend downward, so that it forms a sort of chair shape. If you drew a series of evenly spaced rings around the root and stem with india ink before you turned the seedling on its side, you would find that both the root and the stem turned by growing more on one side than on the other. Scientists have found that this kind of growth is controlled by a chemical that flows through the plant from its growing tips. In both animals and plants, controlling and regulating chemicals are known as hormones. This plant growth hormone has been named *auxin* (meaning "helper").

Sprouting seeds can be observed most readily by growing them on a moist blotter. But if you want to continue the growth of the seedlings, they should be planted in soil. For plants take in not only water but also

dissolved minerals and other substances through their roots. And beans, as legumes, can form nodules and play host to nitrogen-fixing bacteria only if they grow in soil that contains these bacteria.

Partners in the Roots

The partnership between legumes and nitrogen-fixing bacteria was first discovered back in 1888, by two German botanists named Hellriegel and Wilfarth. Their experiment was a very simple one, which is easy for you to repeat with bean plants. They planted one set of seeds in sterile sand. (You can make a sample of sand sterile by heating it in a hot oven for an hour to kill bacteria. Don't use a plastic container that might melt!) For another batch of seeds they took fertile soil in which legumes had been grown successfully, added water, stirred, and then filtered off the solid particles of soil. They added the liquid *extract* obtained in this way to another portion of sterile sand and planted seeds in it. The legumes grown in sterile sand did not grow well, and no nodules formed on their roots. The legumes grown in the sand enriched with soil extract grew well and formed nodules.

It has been found since then that there are about seven different kinds of nodule bacteria, each of which grows in the roots of a different kind of legume. The nitrogen-fixing bacteria that live in the nodules of pea roots will not grow in the roots of clover or alfalfa, those of soybeans will not grow in snap bean roots, and so on. Seed companies sell cultures of nodule bacteria for each kind of crop, which can be used to treat the seeds before planting. If you can obtain a culture for beans, you can try planting one batch of seeds untreated and another treated with the nodule bacteria. Repeat the experiment both in sand and in soil and see which variation grows best. In another experiment, you might try adding various amounts of lime and fertilizers to sand or to soil. Always plant another batch of seeds under exactly the same conditions *except* for the one you are studying, so that you will have a "control" with which to compare the effects of your experiment.

Bean Plants Need Light

From the time the young sprout first pokes its hypocotyl out of the soil, light plays a very important role in its life. Plant two batches of seeds in pots of soil. Place one pot in a dark closet. Place the other on a sunny windowsill. You will find that the plants in the sun turn green soon after they emerge from the soil. (How soon? Time it. Do all the seedlings turn green in the same time after sprouting?) Their cells are manufacturing the green pigment chlorophyll. But the shoots in the dark closet stay a pale yellowish white, even though they look normal otherwise.

Light is so important to plants that they can even turn their leaves and bend their stems so that the largest possible leaf surface is exposed to the light. A movie made by time-lapse photography would show the plants in a garden turning to follow the sun as its position in the sky changes from morning to evening. If you place a strong light to the side of a bean plant, it will bend toward the light. (How long does this take?) If you then turn the pot around so that the plant is bending away from the light, it will soon bend to face the light again. This kind of reaction is called *phototropism* ("light-turning"). As in geotropism, the movement of the plant is produced by greater growth on one side than on the other, and it is controlled by the growth hormone auxin.

Day and Night

In most parts of the world, the sun does not shine twenty-four hours a day. As the earth rotates on its axis, periods of light and darkness alternate to give us day and night. Because the earth's axis is tilted slightly, different parts of the world receive different amounts of sunlight in each 24-hour period, and the length of the days and nights changes with the seasons. (Days are longer in the summer and shorter in the winter.) Scientists have found that for many plants, flowering will not begin until the length of the days and nights is just right. Some plants flower when the days are short and will not bloom when the days are long. (Poinsettias, which bloom at Christmastime, are *short-day plants*.) Other plants are *long-day plants*, which will not bloom until the summer when the days are long, even if they are started very early indoors, in a hothouse. Some plants are *day-neutral*: they will bloom when they have reached a certain stage of development, no matter how short or long the days are.

The timing of the blooming of many plants to the length of the days and nights is part of a sort of inner calendar, which helps to keep them in tune with the seasons. Usually the short-day and long-day plants bloom at the day-length that is characteristic of the right part of the growing season in the part of the world where they originated. But plants have spread from one part of the world to another, and man has helped to speed up this process by carrying useful plants like beans about with him on his travels.

Many of the New World beans are believed to have originated in Central America, near the equator. Days are shorter there than they are during the summer growing season in the temperate regions, such as the United States. Many varieties of beans are short-day plants: they will not flower during the summer up north. There are some day-neutral bean plants, and, as you might expect, these are the varieties that have been used to breed most of the commercial beans grown today. But some of the pole beans are short-day varieties, and some of the semi-pole varieties are affected by the day-length in a different way: they are bushy in short day-lengths and twining in long day-lengths.

Test several different varieties of beans to determine whether their flowering is affected by the length of the days and nights. Try growing some batches with eight hours of light a day, some with ten, twelve, fourteen, eighteen, and twenty-four hours of light a day. Your local newspaper probably lists the times of sunrise and sunset in your area. You can artificially lengthen the day for some of your experimental plants by placing them under strong artificial lights for a set number of hours each day after the sun stops shining on them. You can create an artificial short day by removing the plants to a dark closet after they have received their day's quota of sunlight. (You can run the whole experiment under artificial lights if you prefer. The usual light bulbs do not give out all the radiations plants need to grow well. Special fluorescent lamps for plant growing are sold. Or a mixture of fluorescent lamps and incandescent bulbs can be used.)

Beans follow the daily cycles of day and night in another interesting way. If you watch a bean plant carefully, you will notice that it holds its leaves out broadly during the day, but droops them and folds them slightly at night. These cycles of leaf movements occur regularly, every 24-hour cycle. Scientists call them "sleep movements." Are the beans' sleep movements determined by the presence and absence of light, or are they timed by a sort of "inner clock"? Try growing some bean plants under lights around the clock to see whether they show the usual sleep movements. Continue the experiment for a week to see if there are any changes.

How Plants Grow

Many other experiments can be conducted with growing beans. For example, if you measure the height of a bean seedling every day from the time it first sprouts up out of the soil, and then plot the daily measurements on graph paper, you will find that you are drawing a sort of S-shaped curve. The bean seedling starts slowly, then has a sudden spurt, when the curve almost seems to climb straight up the paper, then levels off and hardly grows at all. The same kind of curve will be repeated with any seedling you pick (unless it gets sick). Not only that, but scientists have found that the same kind of S-shaped curve is obtained for growing animals.

As you grow beans, you will think of other experiments to try. Whenever you think "what would happen if . . ."—try it, and see. Keep careful records of what you do, and whenever possible, try to vary only one condition (such as temperature, light, minerals) at a time. You may even discover something about plants that no one has ever known before.

BEANS FOR GOOD EATING

"Dry beans—the best buy in the meat group," begins a leaflet for consumers published by the U.S. Department of Agriculture. And with meat prices rising higher and higher, many families are rediscovering how versatile and nutritious beans can be.

Like meats, dried beans are high in proteins. About 21 to 25 percent of the weight of dried kidney beans, navy beans, and most other bean varieties is protein, while dried soybeans are more than 35 percent protein. (The values for soybean meal and concentrates are even higher.) Beans also provide vitamins, particularly B vitamins, and important minerals such as iron, copper, manganese, molybdenum, and magnesium. It is estimated that one cup of cooked dried red beans provides about 230 calories and about a quarter of the minimum amount of protein needed by an adult each day, a quarter of the minimum daily amount of iron for a woman (and 46 percent of the daily minimum for a man), and large amounts of the B vitamins thiamin and riboflavin. Fresh snap beans are nutritious, too. Though they do not contain as large a proportion of protein as dried beans, they are rich sources of vitamin A, vitamin C, and the B vitamins.

Ways to serve beans are almost unlimited. They are good not only as vegetable "side dishes," but also in main-dish casseroles, salads, and snacks. There are so many different kinds of beans and different ways to prepare them that you could serve bean dishes for lunch and dinner all week and not repeat yourself once. (In Boston it is traditional to eat baked beans for breakfast, while in Japan soybean paste soup is just as popular a drink as coffee is in the West.)

Buying Beans

Unless you are growing your own beans, the first step in getting them to the table is buying them. Snap beans are sold either fresh, canned, or frozen. (Frozen green beans are usually "cut" into short pieces or "French style"—cut lengthwise into strips.) When buying fresh green beans, look for a fresh appearance in the vegetable bins. The beans should be clean, firm but tender, free from scars, and well-shaped. Try to select beans of about the same stage of ripeness, so that they will all cook at the same rate. (If you cook beans of different stages together, the very young pods will be overdone and the old ones underdone when the rest of the beans are just right.)

Dried beans are sold in bags or boxes, usually by the pound. Some of the dried beans sold in the stores have been inspected by federal, state, or private inspectors. But usually the grade is not marked on the package. You can be your own "bean inspector," by watching for the same kinds of things the federal and state inspectors do.

First of all, try to buy beans in cellophane packages, or in boxes with "see-through" windows. Examine the beans, looking for the following things:

1. *Bright colors.* The beans should have bright, uniform colors. If the colors are pale, this may mean that the beans have been stored for a long time and are no longer fresh. Although they are still nutritious, they will take longer to cook.

2. *Uniform size.* If the beans are of different sizes, they will not cook evenly. (Small beans cook faster than large ones.)

3. *Defects.* Look for cracked seed

coats, stones and other bits of foreign material, and pinholes caused by insect damage—these are signs of low-quality beans.

Be sure to read the label on the package. It must contain the name and address of the manufacturer, packer, or distributor, the name of the product (such as navy beans, Great Northern beans, etc.), and the weight in pounds and ounces. The label may also contain other interesting and useful information, such as a picture of a suggested way to serve the beans and recipes for bean dishes.

After you buy dry beans, you can store them in a cool, dry place for several months without any loss of quality. Keep the beans in the original package as long as it is unopened. (Don't buy a package with a hole or slit in it!) After opening, dry beans should be stored in a container with a tight-fitting lid. Don't mix leftovers of packages bought at different times, because older beans take longer to cook than fresher ones.

Beans are also sold in cans in various prepared forms. One of the most popular is baked beans (with or without pork). Canned baked beans can be heated and served as a side dish with frankfurters or other meat dishes. (Remember that canned baked beans are already cooked. To prepare them for eating, all that is needed is a brief heating in a pot, until they are at the right temperature for good taste.) Canned baked beans can also be used with other ingredients in a variety of casseroles and other main dishes.

Green Bean Recipes

Fresh green beans are cooked most often by boiling. Use the smallest possible amount of water to prevent the beans from burning. If you cook beans (like other vegetables) in too much water, you will lose valuable vitamins in the cooking water. Salt the water lightly and bring it to a boil before you add the beans. The beans can be cooked whole, snapped into short bite-size pieces, or sliced French style, using the attachment on the top of a potato peeler. Cook the beans just until they are tender, and serve right away. (If fresh green beans are rewarmed, they turn color and lose their fresh taste.)

Frozen green beans are cooked in the same way, except that cooking times are shorter than for fresh beans.

For some added taste interest, you can add sliced almonds, mushrooms, or tiny pearl onions to the beans while they are cooking. Beans are also good with carrots. For example, try this recipe:

Dilly Carrots and Beans
      ¾ cup water
      1 teaspoon sugar
      ½ teaspoon salt
      ½ teaspoon dill seed
      ½ pound green snap beans, fresh
      4 carrots, medium-sized
      ¼ cup Italian dressing

Mix the water, sugar, salt, and dill seed in a saucepan, and bring to boiling. Wash and trim the green beans but leave them whole. Add to the boiling water, and simmer for 5 minutes. Cut the carrots into thin strips, 2 to 3 inches long, and add to the green beans. Boil about 10 minutes, until both carrots and beans are tender and the liquid is almost evaporated. Add Italian dressing and toss to mix well. Serve hot, or chill and use in tossed vegetable salads. Makes six servings.

Green beans are also good in vegetable soups, stews, and baked in casseroles with meat or cheese. For example:

Green Beans with Cheese
      1½ pounds snap beans
      ⅓ cup cream or evaporated milk
      ½ cup grated cheese
      Salt
      Paprika
      Butter

Wash and trim beans. Steam in boiling water for about 5 minutes. Drain. Arrange in a greased casserole. Sprinkle with salt, paprika, ⅓ cup cream, and ⅓ cup grated cheese. Toss lightly to blend the cheese and beans. Dot with butter and sprinkle with the remaining cheese. Bake in a hot (400°F) oven for 15-20 minutes. Makes six servings.

Lima Bean Recipes

Lima beans are sold fresh, frozen, canned, and dried. Fresh or frozen, they need only a short boiling or steaming, while canned lima beans need only be warmed up. For an authentic American Indian dish, mix lima beans with corn and serve as succotash. Lima beans are also good in casseroles, for example:

Lima Bean Casserole
- 10 ounce package lima beans, frozen, cooked
- ½ cup milk
- 10½ ounce can cheese soup, condensed
- 1 cup celery, diced
- ¼ cup parsley, finely chopped
- 3½ ounce can French fried onion rings

Preheat oven to 350°F (moderate). Grease a 1½ quart casserole. Blend the milk and soup. Add celery, parsley, and lima beans. Place the mixture in the casserole, top with onion rings, and bake 45 minutes. Makes six servings.

Dried Bean Recipes

There is a trick to preparing dried beans: they should be soaked first, to cut down the cooking time. Two soaking methods are recommended. The old method is to place the beans in a large pot or kettle the night before you plan to prepare them, add water (about 3 quarts of water to 1 pound of dried beans), and soak overnight. Modern cooks cut down the soaking time by bringing the water with the beans slowly to a boil and simmering gently for about 2 minutes. Then the heat is turned off, and the beans are allowed to stand for 1 to 2 hours. Then they are ready to cook. (Actually, it is a good idea to boil dry beans for two minutes first even if you do plan to soak them overnight; the boiling prevents them from turning sour, which might happen if they are soaked in a warm room.)

In cooking dry beans, usually a teaspoon of salt for each cup of dry beans is used. In planning meals with beans, remember that beans swell as they soak. One cup of dry beans gives 2 to 2¾ cups of cooked beans. Different types of beans cook at different rates. Black-eyed peas cook the fastest, while black beans, kidney beans, pinto beans, and soybeans take the longest.

Once the beans are soaked and ready to cook, you can do various things with them. Here is a recipe for a basic bean soup:

Bean Soup

1 cup dry beans
6 cups water
1 teaspoon salt
1 ham bone
1 onion

Add salt and ham bone to soaked beans. Cover and cook over low heat for 2 hours. Chop the onion, add to soup, and cook for about 30 minutes more, until the beans are soft. Remove the bone before serving the soup. Makes four servings.

You can get very different tastes by adding various other vegetables to the basic soup recipe: carrots, celery, tomatoes, cabbage, etc. Minestrone is a vegetable soup popular in Italy, which usually contains beans, potatoes, onions, celery, tomatoes, and grated Parmesan cheese.

The traditional Boston dish, baked beans, is made with navy beans:

Baked Beans

2 cups dry navy beans
6 cups water
1 teaspoon salt
¼ pound salt pork, cut in pieces
¼ cup molasses
½ teaspoon dry mustard

After the beans have been soaked, add salt. Then simmer the beans for 45 minutes in the soaking water. Add salt pork and boil gently 30 to 45 minutes longer, until the beans are tender. Meanwhile, preheat the oven to 350°F (moderate). Mix the molasses and mustard and stir the mixture into the beans. Put the beans into a beanpot or 2-quart casserole. Bake for 1 hour, or until tender and lightly browned on top. Check the beanpot from time to time and add a little hot water if the beans seem dry. Makes six servings.

Soybeans can be used in place of the navy beans, to provide even more protein. Soybeans need longer cooking before baking, and then must be baked for 2 hours. (Keep covered for the first 1½ hour, then remove the cover and bake for another 30 minutes to brown the top.)

Some interesting variations on the baked beans recipe can be achieved by mixing ½ cup chopped onions into the beans before baking, or adding ¼ cup catsup, 1 tablespoon worcestershire sauce, and ½ teaspoon ginger. Brown sugar or maple syrup can be used in place of molasses.

If you want to use beans as a meat substitute, you might try the following recipe for beanburgers:

Beanburgers

    2 cups cooked dry beans
    1 egg
      Fine dry bread crumbs
      Fat or oil for frying

Mash beans. Beat the egg and add to mashed beans. Shape into patties and roll in bread crumbs. Fry in fat until brown on both sides. Makes four servings.

As variations, you can mix browned, chopped onion, ground beef, and catsup with the beans before shaping into patties, and bake (at 350°F) or fry. Place the patties on the lower half of a hamburger roll and top with a slice of cheese; place in a 300°F oven until the cheese just melts, to make bean cheeseburgers.

In Mexico the black beans called frijoles negros are eaten in a number of ways. Sometimes they are served whole:

Kabach

    1 pound black beans
    1 teaspoon salt
    2 onions
    6 cups water
    ½ cup oil or bacon fat

Soak beans as usual. Then cover the soaked beans to a level about 1 inch above the beans, add salt and a small onion, and boil until the beans are easily pierced by a fork. Fry a medium-sized onion in oil or bacon fat until golden brown and add to the platter of beans when serving. Makes six servings.

Sometimes the frijoles are refried:

Frijoles Refritos, ("refried beans")
- 1 pound black beans
- 1 teaspoon salt
- 2 onions
- 6 cups water
- ½ cup oil or bacon fat

Soak beans as usual and boil as for ka-bach. When the beans are tender, mash them thoroughly in a little of their own broth, or place beans and broth in a blender and blend until smooth. Chop a small onion and brown in oil or bacon fat until golden brown. Add mashed or blended beans and fry at medium-low heat, stirring frequently to prevent sticking. Continue to fry until the beans thicken sufficiently to form a loaf. Garnish the loaf with pieces of fried tortillas or Fritos. Makes six servings.

Another Mexican bean dish, chili con carne ("chili with meat"), has become quite popular in the United States as well. In a consumer survey in the San Francisco area in 1970, chili was reported as the most popular bean dish. (Bean soup was second, and pork and beans third.) Chili con carne is usually made with kidney beans or pinto beans:

Chili Con Carne
  2 cups cooked red kidney beans or pinto beans
  1 pound ground beef
  2 cups cooked tomatoes or canned tomato puree
  1 onion
  ½ teaspoon chili powder
  1 teaspoon salt
  1 tablespoon fat or oil

Chop onion and brown in fat. Add the remaining ingredients, mix, cover, and simmer for 20 minutes on medium-low heat. Add water if the mixture becomes too dry. Makes six servings.

After you have tried these bean dishes, you will find more tasty and interesting recipes on the labels of bean packages and in the following pamphlets and book:
Vegetables in Family Meals, Home and Garden Bulletin No. 105, U.S. Department of Agriculture, 1971. (For sale by the Superintendent of Documents, U.S. Government Printing Office, Washington, D.C. 20402, 20 cents.)
Take a Can of Beans, Campbell Soup Company. (Write to Consumer Service Division, Campbell Soup Company, Camden, N.J. 08101.)
Selected Ritter Recipes, P. J. Ritter Company. (Write to P. J. Ritter Division of Curtice-Burns, Inc., Bridgeton, N.J. 08302.)

Favorite Green Bean Recipes; Favorite Lima Bean Recipes; Van Camp's Pork and Beans, Stokely-Van Camp, Inc. (Write to Home Economics Department, Stokely-Van Camp, Inc., Indianapolis, Indiana.)

Margaret and Ancel Keys, *The Benevolent Bean,* Farrar, Straus and Giroux, New York, 1972. $5.95; paperback $2.45.

BEAN GAMES
AND CRAFTS

For many centuries, the Indians of the American Southwest have played a game with their favorite bean, the tepary. The seeds of this bean ripen in a variety of colors. Three colors are used in the game: white, black, and yellow. The game is played by two players. Each player starts with ten white beans, ten black beans, and one yellow bean. The first player puts one bean of each color into a gourd, shakes it vigorously, and then tosses the beans out. The yellow bean tells who wins the toss: if it falls closer to the black bean than the white one, the player must give both the white bean and the black one to his opponent. If the yellow bean has

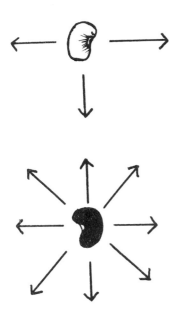

landed closer to the white bean, the opponent gives the player a white bean and a black one. (Each player always keeps his own yellow bean.) The two players continue to toss their beans out in turn until one of them has all the white and black beans. He is the winner.

This ancient Indian game is still fun and easy to play. You can use three different kinds of dried beans that can be bought in a grocery store or supermarket—for example, navy beans (white), red or pink beans, and pinto beans (spotted). A paper cup can be used in place of the gourd for shaking the beans.

Indeed, a few packages of dried beans can provide many hours of fun in games and other activities. You can use different-colored beans as markers in hopscotch, and as counters in various board games, such as Monopoly.

Beans can also be used in many games that are played with marbles. Chinese checkers is one of these. Another type of game board that you can make for yourself is shown in the drawing on page 79. Use a large piece of cardboard and draw the lines as shown, an inch apart. Punch a hole in the cardboard (with a large nail or a pencil point) at each point shown by an o in the drawing. With this board, and a bag of

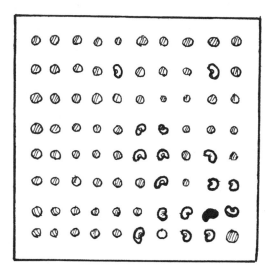

beans, you can play two different games.

The first is a game for two players, called *Fox and Geese*. In the line drawing at the top, the board is set up for the beginning of the game. One player has seventeen white beans. The other player has a single colored bean. (To determine which player will have the white beans and which the colored bean, place a white bean and a colored bean in a bag, and have one player pull out one of them without looking.)

The white beans represent the geese, while the colored bean is the fox. The fox can move a single space in any direction, forward, back, to either side, and diagonally. He can also jump over a single goose into an empty space, as in checkers. If a fox jumps

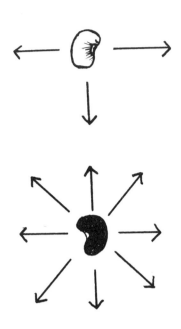

over a goose, the goose is "killed" and is removed from the board immediately. Just as in checkers, the fox can jump over a series of geese if there are single empty spaces between them, and thus he can kill more than one goose in one move.

The geese cannot jump over the fox, and they can move only sideways or forward, not backward or diagonally.

The player with the fox moves first, and then the moves alternate. (The player with the geese can move only one goose at a time.) The fox tries to kill all the geese, while the geese try to crowd the fox in a corner. If the fox is trapped so that he cannot move, the geese win the game. If he succeeds in removing all the geese before they can trap him, he wins.

The drawing shows the board for a solitaire game, to be played by one person. Any color beans can be used. All the holes are filled except the middle one. The object is to move one bean at a time, either a single space or jumping as in checkers, until only one bean remains. (The jumped beans are removed from the board.) The last bean should be in the center hole. In this game, a bean can never move diagonally, only vertically or horizontally.

80

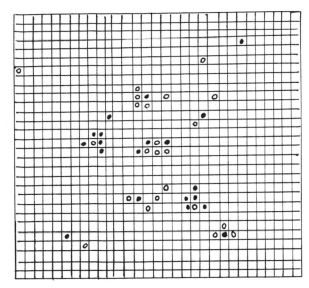

Other problems can be set in bean solitaire: for example, leave the space in the upper left corner open and try to move the beans so that only one remains, in the lower right corner.

Beans are also good to use for some board games played on a pattern of squares like a checkerboard. On a large piece of cardboard, draw a pattern of squares in indelible ink. Make the lines one inch apart. There should be 31 squares across and 29 squares down. You can use larger or smaller numbers if you like, but both should be odd numbers. Now, with beans of two different colors (such as white navy beans and red kidney beans or black beans), you are ready to play *Bean Go*. This game was first invented in

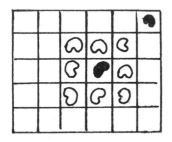

China, about four thousand years ago. The Chinese called it Wei-Chi, but when the game was sent to Japan in the year A.D. 754, the Japanese named their version Igo, from which the modern name of "Go" is taken.

The game is started by placing a bean in one of the squares. (In some variations of Go, stones or seeds are placed on the intersections of lines, rather than the open spaces between them, but otherwise the rules of play are similar.) One player has all colored beans, the other all white beans. A dark-colored bean always goes first, and it can be placed anywhere on the board the player wishes. Then the player with white beans places one on a square on the board—again, anywhere he wishes, except on a square already occupied. As the game proceeds, each player in turn places another bean in a square on the board. Each tries to surround one or more of his opponent's beans with a continuous ring of beans of his own color. If he succeeds, he has "captured" the surrounded beans and removes them from the board. Once placed on the board, a bean is never moved again unless it is captured. Play continues until there are no more moves to be made. Each player's score is the number of his beans on the board, minus the number of his beans that have been captured.

A Go board can also be used for another two-player game called *Five Beans in a Row*. Again, one player has all colored beans and the other all white beans. This time the object is to place five beans of the same color in a row in any direction. As in tic-tac-toe, you must try to line up your own beans while blocking your opponent's attempts.

Bean Hole Toss can be played with beans of two colors and some holes scooped out in the ground. This game is popular with children in many countries of the world. In a variation played in West Africa, a cup-sized hole is dug in the ground. Then a throwing line is scratched out about three to five feet from the hole. (The exact distance depends on the age of the children and their skill at bean tossing.)

This variation of Bean Hole Toss is played by three players. Each of two players starts out with fifteen beans. The first player holds all his beans in his hand and tosses them at the hole, trying to get as many in as possible. The second player then takes his turn. The beans of each color in the hole are counted, and then the third player picks up all the scattered beans that have fallen outside the hole and takes his turn with those. The player to get the most beans in the hole is the winner.

One variation of beanbag toss is called

Haba Gaba, which comes from Spanish words meaning "French bean." It comes from the Sierra Leone region of West Africa. To play Haba Gaba, cut three circular holes in a large board or piece of cardboard, at the top, center, and bottom. The top hole should be two inches in diameter, the middle hole three, and the bottom hole four inches. The largest hole counts for one point, the middle hole for two, and the smallest hole for three points. Set up the board at a forty-five-degree angle (slanting away from the players). Then each player in turn tries to pitch the beanbag through one of the holes. The game is played in innings of eight to ten tosses for each player. The winner is the one who has scored the most points after three innings.

In today's complicated technological world, which is often impersonal and sometimes frightening, handcrafts have become extremely popular. People long to go back to an older, simpler time, and making things of beauty with their own hands, as their great-grandparents did, provides great comfort. Beans, which have been a part of man's history and culture since before the beginning of recorded history, are especially appropriate natural materials for a variety of craft activities, and they are attractive and inexpensive besides.

Like other seeds, beans can be strung into necklaces, bracelets, earrings, and other jewelry. One way to pierce beans for stringing is to soak dried beans for one to three hours (you can determine the exact time by experimenting—it varies with the kind of bean) and then pierce them with a needle. Then dry them, either for a day or two spread out on a table or shelf, or for an hour at the lowest setting in the oven. Select the beans according to color and shape and discard any whose seed coats have split.

Different-shaped beans make good heads and bodies for animals made from bent pipecleaners. (Form a nest for the bean with the pipecleaner and glue the bean in place.) Beans also make good eyes and noses for clay figures.

You can also make bean pictures with an interesting "3D" effect. Spread a thick layer of white glue on a cardboard backing, and then place the beans in it and allow to dry. You can use the beans to form outline pictures. Or you can cover the entire backing with beans, using different colors to produce a mosaic effect.

An old-fashioned craft that is becoming popular again is making a kind of display called a hutch. First you take or build a shallow wooden box, then add short shelves placed at angles or slants to divide the box into an interesting pattern of unequal spaces. Dried seeds and other natural materials, as well as pictures and related objects, are glued into the spaces to form an eye-pleasing arrangement. The feathers, like part of an Indian headdress, and the corn husks and dried corn and beans bring back memories of the old Indian tales of how these life-sustaining plants were first given to man.

INDEX